Original title:
Saturn's Slam Poetry

Copyright © 2025 Creative Arts Management OÜ
All rights reserved.

Author: Theodore Sinclair
ISBN HARDBACK: 978-1-80567-870-0
ISBN PAPERBACK: 978-1-80567-991-2

Galaxy's Gaze

In the vastness of night, where the starlight beams,
Planets chuckle, sharing cosmic dreams.
Jupiter's jokes, they're a gas, it's true,
While Mars rolls its eyes, not amused by the view.

Uranus spins round, with a wink and a twist,
Shouting punchlines through the nebula mist.
A comet zips by with a whoosh and a grin,
'Catch me if you can!'—let the laughs begin!

Black holes invite us to their cosmic dance,
With gravity's pull, we're caught in a trance.
Stars flip and flop, in their twinkling attire,
They're the real entertainers, sparking cosmic fire.

In the galaxy's lounge, where the humor expands,
We toast with the asteroids, our laughter unmanned.
So let's orbit the fun, in this stellar bazaar,
With giggles that echo, from near and afar!

Echoes in the Ether

Floating through space, so light, so free,
Chasing my dreams on a cosmic spree.
Lost in the echoes, I find my cheer,
Dancing with stars, I have no fear.

Ticklish comets whisper a joke,
While asteroids giggle, oh how they poke!
Gravity's pulling, but I just sway,
In this vast theater, I'll laugh and play.

Orbiting Inspirations

Round and round, the planets spin,
With endless giggles, they wear a grin.
The rings of adventure, oh what a sight,
In orbiting chaos, we find delight.

Jupiter's belly laughs, it's quite a show,
While tiny moons dance, putting on a glow.
Gravity's tickle in this joyful race,
We whirl and twirl in this vast, wild space.

The Veil of Atmospheres

Beneath thick clouds, a raucous party,
With breezy banter, it's never hearty.
Neon flashes, and laughter spills,
Through stunning veils, the joy just thrills.

Silly storms chuckle, rainbows in sight,
As lightning bolts crackle, oh what a fright!
But within the chaos, humor's the key,
In this misty world, we laugh and agree.

Galactic Rhymes

Stars pulling pranks in the velvet dark,
Orbital jokes, oh, they leave a mark.
Nebulae twinkle, as if to say,
This rhythmic dance is the cosmic way.

With quasar giggles and supernova cheer,
The universe winks, it's perfectly clear.
In rhymes of the galaxies, we find our groove,
A cosmic freestyle, with nothing to prove.

The Orbiting Wordsmith

In the cosmos, I scribble, with stars in a whirl,
Each comet a punchline, in this dance I twirl.
My quill's made of stardust, my ink's from the sun,
Jokes echo in silence, where space is the fun.

Planets laugh softly, they're my audience tight,
As I drop my puns like meteors at night.
Galaxies chuckle, they jiggle and sway,
While I throw my verses in a cosmic ballet.

Celestial Beats

My heart beats like planets, in a rhythm divine,
With each thump, I'm laughing, like gravity's wine.
I dance through the cosmos, a comet on cue,
Dropping beats like meteors, who knew it was true?

I bounce off the moons, in a hilarious spin,
As satirical stardust brings laughter within.
Creating a buzz while the asteroids cheer,
In the vastness of space, it's the humor I steer.

Shadows of the Gas Giant

In the shade of a giant, I craft my dark gags,
With a swirl of the clouds, I'm out to tease fags.
Each quip's a balloon, inflating like gas,
Making jokes in the shadows, oh what a blast!

I'm riding on winds that are full of surprise,
Tickling the moons with my puns in the skies.
Even the dark matter can't hold back a grin,
As laughter erupts from the depths of the din.

Rhythms of the Rings

These rings are my stage, I strut and I prance,
With a wink to the universe, I'm here for a dance.
My words are like particles, swirling in flight,
Creating a spectacle, a comic delight.

I riff off the rocks, shiny and bright,
Each joke is a glimmer, catching the light.
As meteors scoff, and the stardust spins,
In the vastness of cosmos, my laughter begins.

Intergalactic Inspirations

In the cosmos where the planets spin,
Jokes drift like comets, let's let them in.
With aliens chuckling over cosmic stew,
Laughter echoes in the Milky Way's blue.

Stars twinkle with humor, shining so bright,
Orbiting jokes that take flight at night.
Gravity's got nothing on giggles we've found,
As we dance with the quirks of space all around.

Rhymes of the Radiant Rings

Rings of ice and rock, what a sight to behold,
Who knew they'd harbor stories humorous and bold?
Planets tease each other, shout out their roars,
While moons do the tango, laughing to the core.

In a space bar where beings sip starlight drinks,
Jokes fly faster than light, oh what a wink!
Gravity defying, with puns that just cling,
Witty comments bouncing around on a swing.

A Cosmic Canvas

Brush strokes of stardust paint the night sky,
Creating silly scenes that make us all sigh.
A nebula giggles, suns crack up too,
As colors collide, oh the joy they construe!

From quasar jokes to black hole pranks,
In the cosmic gallery, we give our thanks.
With laughter as bright as supernova's glow,
Each chuckle transcends where we dare not to go.

Starbound Syllables

Waves of sound travel through the deep void,
Beats in the ether, chaotic yet coyed.
Verses tumble like asteroids, bumpy and free,
Rhythms collide in a cosmic spree.

Lightyears of laughter wrapped up in rhyme,
Time flows like a river in whimsical time.
Jokes from the stars, bright and absurd,
In the dance of the cosmos, not a soul is unheard.

An Artist's Orbit

In a canvas wrapped in space,
Brush strokes dance with vibrant grace.
Planets twirl in cosmic jams,
While stars giggle at the clams.

Comets sprint in wild delight,
Chasing meteors in the night.
Paint the sky with silly dreams,
As gravity plays with our beams.

Rings of color, a swirling spree,
Dancing planets shout, "Look at me!"
Artistry in every glance,
The universe joins in the dance.

Jupiter's Shadow and Saturn's Light

Jupiter grins, casting shade,
While Saturn's light is unafraid.
Together they sip cosmic tea,
Sharing laughs with a solar spree.

In the void, a quirky play,
Planets joke, come what may.
With shadows long and laughter wide,
Divine giggles they cannot hide.

Frolicking in gravitational fun,
Racing moons beneath the sun.
In this space where humor ignites,
Witty banter fills the nights.

The Voice Beneath the Atmosphere

Whispers float on gas-filled waves,
Where silence giggles, laughter braves.
A bubble world of sounds entwined,
The cosmos hums, uniquely defined.

Meteor showers laugh and tease,
While swirling winds bring cosmic ease.
Voices rise from depths unknown,
Echoing through realms of stone.

Outside the orbits, jokes abound,
In every planet's spin, they're found.
Playful prose from stars up high,
Makes even black holes crack a sigh.

Starlit Struggles

Twinkling lights with mischief grand,
Stumble through the cosmic land.
Stars collide in playful fights,
Creating dances of sheer delight.

Nebulae stretch with blissful sighs,
As galaxies wink with starry eyes.
Planetary pranks make history,
In timeless glee, they sing their story.

Gravity pulls, but humor lifts,
Amidst the void, it brilliantly shifts.
In this struggle of laughs and bliss,
Every star finds joy in the abyss.

An Ode to the Outer Realm

In the sky, where the gas giants play,
Planets dance in a cosmic ballet.
Neptune jokes with a wink and a spin,
While Pluto insists it's still in the ring.

Rings of rock with a shimmering glow,
A tilt of the axis, put on a show.
Asteroids trip in their space-contained lanes,
The Milky Way giggles as it sways and strains.

Stellar Symphony

Stars gather 'round with their bright, bold tunes,
A cosmic choir serenades the moons.
Mars strums his guitar, oh what a sound!
While Venus provides the harmony around.

Pluto's jokes land like comets on course,
Laughing until we feel the force.
Each orbit a line in this outlandish rhyme,
As the galaxies sway, oh what a time!

Jupiter's Lullaby

Jupiter hums with a spirited cheer,
His moons join in, laying calm in the sphere.
With a stormy twist and a jovial wink,
They sing to the stars, make us pause and think.

From swirling storms to a gentle breeze,
Laughter erupts among galactic trees.
As satellites snooze, we feast on the fun,
The universe sleeps 'til the next day's sun.

Chronos and Chaos

Tick-tock goes time, or is it just play?
Chronos and Chaos dance every day.
One moves in circles, the other in leaps,
Creating a ruckus while the cosmos sleeps.

Galaxies spin like tops in a race,
With a wink and a nod, they hint at their grace.
As the clock hands clash in a comical brawl,
They intertwine, bringing laughter to all.

Moons of Melancholy and Joy

Floating rocks dressed in glow,
Spin with tales of high and low.
Their craters laugh, their shadows weep,
A dance of spirits, secrets keep.

Round and round, they like to tease,
Blowing kisses on cosmic breeze.
One feels blue, the other jest,
Every night, they send their best.

Jovial orbs in endless fight,
Play tag through the starry night.
Crack a smile, let worries slide,
In this ballet, we all reside.

Moons of chaos, moons of cheer,
They whisper wonders in our ear.
With funny quirks and cosmic jest,
Their spinning stories never rest.

Echo Chamber of the Cosmos

In the void where echoes play,
Galaxies laugh in their own way.
What was that? A comet's song?
Or maybe jesters all along?

Every bounce, a cosmic cheer,
Sounding jokes from far yet near.
Asteroids chuckle, pulsars shout,
In this echo, there's no doubt.

Nebulae swirl in vibrant hues,
Colorful gossip, silly news.
They whisper loud and giggle bright,
In this chamber, everything's light.

Sing and shout, for why not try?
Let your laughter leap and fly.
In this universe, bold and grand,
Funny stories, hand in hand.

Nebula Narratives

In clouded realms where colors spin,
Nebulae tease with a cheeky grin.
Painting dreams with their starry dust,
In cosmic battles of wanderlust.

They swirl and jiggle, swirling tales,
With puffs of laughter that never pales.
A story here, a giggle there,
In every hue, a cosmic flare.

They dance like poets on a stage,
Charting the heavens, page by page.
With every twirl, a hearty joke,
In this vast space, joy awoke.

Nebula tales from far-off lands,
Written in light by cosmic hands.
Join the merriment, laugh and play,
In this narrative where stars sway.

The Shout of the Celestial Sphere

Hear the cosmos as it yells,
In every twinkle, laughter swells.
A shout that travels light-years far,
Tickling your soul, like a shooting star.

The planets join in raucous glee,
Sharing secrets from A to Z.
Whispers of quarks, dance of blades,
Through space they rumble, never fades.

Voice of stardust, void of dread,
Funny shouts from the sky ahead.
A celestial choir, boundless cheer,
In every hollow, giggles appear.

So listen close, let spirits sing,
For every moment, joy will bring.
The shout from above, so wild and clear,
In the celestial sphere, we have no fear.

Planetary Pulse

In the dance of the rings, they twirl with glee,
Asteroids chuckle, they're sea-bound, you see.
Stars wink and nod in the cosmic parade,
While planets high-five, not a moment delayed.

Jupiter's jokes shake the Milky Way's core,
Mars cracks a pun, and the laughter does soar.
Uranus rolls over, it's all in good fun,
Even the sun's rays do a shimmy then run.

Venus steals glances, a flirt with the night,
Neptune whispers secrets, a charming delight.
Earth does a moonwalk, it's a sight to behold,
Galactic giggles in the cosmos unfold.

Through the Halo

A halo of laughs, around planets it beams,
On a comet, we ride through each zany dream.
Pluto's a trickster, with a grin oh so sly,
A game of charades in the vast starry sky.

Saturn's rings jingle, like bells on a spree,
While Neptune's deep belly laugh echoes with glee.
Bright meteors dash, with a speedy salute,
While space dust does pirouettes, ever so cute.

Through the cosmic curtain, stars toss confetti,
Witty quips and one-liners, the vibe is so ready.
Galaxies twirl to a cosmic ballet,
Unruly and wild, in a planetary way.

Whirlwinds of Wonder

Spinning and swirling, a cosmic ballet,
Orbits collide in a whimsical way.
Galactic giggles sway with each breeze,
Even the black holes are hard-pressed to tease.

Planets engage in slapstick delight,
Cracking up asteroids, what a sight!
Stars are the audience, popcorn in hand,
A comedy show in the vast cosmic land.

Supernovae burst with a sparkle and pop,
Floating debris can't help but stop.
In this whirlpool of laughter, we float and we spin,
Every crunch and each chuckle, a win-win to win!

The Chorus of the Cosmos

Echoing voices in a stellar duet,
Planets joke about their celestial debt.
"Which one's the hottest?" they bicker and pry,
While the comets just giggle and zoom swiftly by.

The chorus erupts, a rhythm divine,
Bouncing off meteors, every word, every line.
The moons join the fun, in harmony they sing,
While asteroids dance in a cheeky ring.

Squares, rectangles and triangles too,
Making shapes out of laughter amidst the blue.
Space is alive with whimsy and cheer,
In this universe, laughter is the frontier.

Cosmic Chronicles

In the depths of space, I lost my sock,
Floating in zero-gravity, what a shock.
Aliens giggle as I do the twist,
My laundry's in orbit, can't believe this list.

Jupiter's dance floor, a gas giant thrill,
With balloons of helium, we all get our fill.
Galactic DJ spinning records of light,
Dance-offs with comets, oh what a sight!

Mars brought the cupcakes, the frosting was red,
Had to explain why the frosting was spread.
We laughed 'til we cried, our faces turned green,
Space parties are wild, it's the best you've seen.

In orbits we swirl, we take every chance,
Asteroids waltz as we join in the dance.
With satellites cheering us, the moon starts to sway,
The universe beams, hip-hip-hooray!

The Silence Between Stars

They say silence is golden, but let's not forget,
The awkwardness lingers, like a cosmic duet.
Stars stare expectantly, their giggles suppressed,
As we float in the void, feeling quite blessed.

Whispers of stardust, a tickle on my skin,
I trip over neutron stars, trying to spin.
The cosmos is watching, it holds its breath tight,
Wondering if it's us, or if it's just night.

Do planets get bored? Do they count little moons?
I asked a bright comet, it hummed some tunes.
'Oh yes,' it replied, 'we dance to the beat,
Of cosmic confusion, it's quite a treat.'

The jokes we share travel at lightspeed so fast,
In the laughter of galaxies, I'm never outclassed.
So here in the silence, let's savor the jest,
In the space between stars, humor's the best.

Planetary Prose

Oops! I spilled my drink on the rings of a king,
The Saturnian vibe, oh what chaos they bring.
A laugh from a moonlet, it wobbles delight,
In the playground of planets, we stay up all night.

Venus plays 'Truth or Dare' with a wink in her eye,
While Mercury's racing, oh my, oh my!
Mars claims he's the strongest, a feat to digest,
But his cookies are soft; who knew he was stressed?

We've got black holes pulling us into a whirl,
While cosmic clowns comically twist and twirl.
The sun's got jokes that brighten the day,
In the solar system, we jest, laugh and play.

Earth rolls her eyes, but she can't help but grin,
Every pun in the cosmos is a win-win-win.
So join in the fun, let the laughter be free,
In this tale of planets, there's joy, can't you see?

Harmonic Horizons

Under the arch of cosmic delight,
We strum on the strings of the starry night.
Harmonies giggle while planets all sway,
Their laughter a tune that carries away.

Asteroids bubble, with giggles and gas,
As I tap on their surface, they rattle and pass.
"Who's got the rhythm?" a satellite cries,
As music spills over from Jupiter's skies.

Tune into the echoes of meteors' flight,
They whistle a tune that can ignite.
Beneath glittery skies, constellations align,
Their silly expressions are truly divine.

So tune in to laughter, let's sing to the stars,
Join me in dance 'neath the cosmic guitars.
As harmonies linger and twinkle with flair,
In this universe grand, let's spread joy everywhere!

Celestial Strains

Planets sway, a cosmic joke,
Dancing dust in a celestial cloak.
Rings of laughter, oh what a sight,
Orbiting whimsy, day and night.

Meteor showers, punchlines fly,
Stars chuckle softly, oh my, oh my!
Gravity's pull, a playful tease,
Galactic giggles, float on the breeze.

Asteroids bounce, they skip and hop,
In the void where the comets plop.
Laughter echoes through the dark,
As cosmic voices find their spark.

A universe of jests unplanned,
In the silent depths, we all understand.
With every twinkle from afar,
The cosmos chuckles, there you are!

The Music of the Milky Way

Hear the whispers of the night,
Galaxies hum, what pure delight!
A symphony of shooting stars,
Tickling the void, strumming guitars.

Spaceships dance to a jazzy beat,
Solar winds sway, oh so sweet!
Planets clap their hands in glee,
While the asteroids tap, can't you see?

From black holes, echoes of cheer,
Comets join in, let's lend an ear!
Constellations wink, don't be late,
In this cosmic fête, let's celebrate!

Playful tunes from afar can call,
While stars jiggle, they never fall.
Join the chorus of moonlit rays,
Beneath the laughter of the Milky Way!

Titan's Timbre

On Titan's shores, the bubbles pop,
Paddling starlight, never stop.
Waves of giggles roll ashore,
In a sea that tickles evermore.

Methane rivers sing a tune,
Bubbling softly beneath the moon.
The sky wears a grin, it's clear to see,
As Titans dance in revelry.

Radio signals bouncing high,
Cosmic jokes that never die.
Floating on clouds of surf and fun,
In this world, we're all just one.

Echoes of laughter fill the air,
In this moonlit realm, without a care.
So join the fun, don't be shy,
Let's make some music as we fly!

Woven in the Weave of Time

Time's a trickster, can't you see?
Spinning tales quite whimsically.
Chronicles tangle, laughter flows,
Each tick-tock hides a joke that glows.

Years weave patterns thick and thin,
Laugh lines match the journeys within.
Past and future, a dance divine,
In cosmic fabric, all intertwined.

Wizards of time, they pull the strings,
Jesters play tunes with vibrant flings.
Moments flutter like butterflies,
Tickling fates beneath the skies.

So let us twirl in this endless mime,
As laughter rings through the weave of time.
Each second, a chuckle, bright and true,
In the grand mosaic, me and you!

Galactic Voices Unfurl

In a cosmic bar, stars sip on light,
Dancing dust bunnies in the endless night.
Planets juggle moons with gleeful grace,
While comets race by, just to keep pace.

Asteroids laugh, throwing jokes with flair,
Gravity chuckles, saying, "Come, share!"
Nebulas swirl in a vibrant spree,
Painting the dark with pure jubilee.

Orbiting thoughts like satellites spin,
Where even the suns break into a grin.
Lightyears stretch but cannot keep still,
In the universe's heart, there's always a thrill.

So raise a glass to the cosmic chorus,
Echoing vibes that are simply porous.
From black holes that swallow all of our woes,
To laughter that flows where the stardust glows.

Cosmic Echoes

In the void, a quasar cracks a smile,
Making light years dance, just for a while.
Planets tell tales of their wild trips,
While sending winked signals with playful flips.

A moon takes a selfie, stars in the back,
Lighting up galaxies with cosmic knack.
Gravity brings the party, weightless and bright,
Where everyone twirls in the soft starlight.

Shooting stars know all the best bars,
Sipping on stardust beneath the soft stars.
Galactic puns orbit, with spells like charms,
No one's too heavy in this space of arms.

So come join the fun, in the stellar sea,
With heaps of laughter, joy, and glee.
Cosmic echoes bounce, like a ball in flight,
In the grand tapestry where all ignites.

Rings of Resilience

Around the giant, the rings spin round,
Making music that's earth-shatteringly sound.
With ice and rock, they form a show,
Dancing through the void, just like a pro.

Every particle's a part of the jam,
Booming like beats in a cosmic slam.
Jupiter winks with his storms on tap,
While Saturn's rings dance, take a bow, clap!

Comedy spills from the comet's tail,
As laughter trails bright through the cosmic veil.
Each loop a laugh, each spin a cheer,
For in the vastness, it's fun we revere.

So let's toast the resilience in every spin,
In the universe's heart, the giggles begin.
With celestial rhythms and jokes that soar,
Let's swirl with the cosmos, forever explore!

Celestial Verses

Twinkling stars pen lines in the dark,
Writing up jokes with a brilliant spark.
Galaxies giggle, with laughter at play,
Twirling through time, in a whimsical way.

In the vastness, each star is a bard,
Spitting out rhymes that hit hard, yet are marred.
A neutron star flexes, showing off might,
While black holes swallow humor with delight.

Solar winds carry tales that enthrall,
Whispering secrets where echoes enthrall.
The Milky Way hums a fantastic tune,
Fueling dreams that lift us to the moon.

So let's share the joy of this cosmic flow,
Where every spark dances, we're never too low.
In the rhythms of space, let our spirits rise,
Finding laughter and hope in the endless skies.

Gravity and Grace

In the cosmos, I take a dive,
Floating feathers, I just survive,
Tripped on stardust, what a chase,
Tumbling planets, just in case.

My dance is wobbly, but so my aim,
I end up here, mixing up the game,
With a twist and twirl, I take my flight,
In zero gravity, it's quite a sight.

Falling up, my friends all stare,
Cosmic capers fill the air,
Laughing comets zooming by,
Bouncing moons, oh me, oh my!

So here I float, a laugh in space,
No graceful exit, I lose my place,
Yet in this chaos, joy takes space,
I'm a funny star in the cosmic race.

Voices of the Vast

Echoes bounce off celestial walls,
Whispers twirl as the galaxy calls,
The moon missed its cue, laughed at the sun,
While the stars giggled, they'd just begun.

Voices blend in a cosmic choir,
Silly puns that never tire,
The Milky Way's wit is hard to beat,
As meteors dance to a groovy beat.

Gravity's got no time for frowns,
Even Uranus grins, wearing crowns,
Comets shout their tales on high,
While constellations wink and sigh.

So let's toast with a cosmic cheer,
To all the voices we hold dear,
In this endless night, oh what a blast,
With laughter echoing, the fun will last.

Nebulous Narratives

In clouds of gas, I spin a tale,
With every twist, I aim to sail,
A swirling mass of jokes and puns,
Nebulae chuckle, oh what fun!

Starry nights beneath a veil,
Whispered dreams that never pale,
I spilled my coffee on a quasar's floor,
And black holes laughed, wanting more.

Planetary friendships, quite absurd,
With asteroid jokes that often blurred,
My stories drift through cosmic haze,
Where even time forgets to phrase.

So gather 'round, my twinkling friends,
Let's weave some laughs that never end,
In this nebula of diverse delight,
We'll laugh and spin beneath starlight.

Harmonies of the Haven

In the sanctuary of the stars,
Music flutters, catching cars,
The harmony of space's jest,
Tickles all, leaves none possessed.

Uplifted by a solar breeze,
We share our jokes, such cosmic keys,
With notes that dance on cosmic waves,
In this haven, laughter saves.

Harmonies soar beyond the moon,
As planets hum a playful tune,
Singing tales of galactic flair,
Where fun and friendships fill the air.

So let us sway to the universal beat,
In this cosmic haven, life's a treat,
With giggles shared at every chance,
Let's twirl through space in a silly dance.

Reverb of the Rings

Planets whirl and dance around,
Laughter echoes, joyful sound.
Rings of ice like hula hoops,
Dancing stars, celestial troops.

Giggles bounce from rock to rock,
Asteroids with their secret clock.
Jupiter rolls his eyes with glee,
While Saturn's rings shout, "Look at me!"

Moons play tag in cosmic air,
Floating softly without a care.
We all cheer and join the fray,
In the skies where the comets sway.

The stars wink knowingly up high,
With jokes hidden in the night sky.
Grab your space shoes, it's time to prance,
In this universe, we all dance.

Harmonies from the Heavens

Orbits sing a merry tune,
Planets jive beneath the moon.
Galaxies strum their starlit lyres,
While comets dance around like fires.

Neptune hums a cheeky beat,
As asteroids shuffle on nimble feet.
Echoes bubble from the void,
The cosmos winks, never coyed.

Mars cracks jokes to lighten the weight,
While Venus twirls, a dazzling fate.
Interstellar laughter rolls,
Harmonics flutter, touch our souls.

In this vast celestial play,
Life's a song, come what may.
Join the chorus, shout and sing,
In the heavens, joy's our king.

Cosmic Confluence

Stars collide in a blaze of flair,
Gravity's pull, a cosmic affair.
Shooting stars trade cheeky glances,
Winking notions lead to dances.

Galactic jokes on cosmic screens,
Universe giggles in gleaming beams.
Wormholes stretch, creating space,
For all of us to join the race.

From Jupiter's belly, laughter bursts,
In this realm where fun never thirsts.
Planets tease with playful pings,
Creating chaos, joy it brings.

Light-years away, yet close at hand,
In this wild, whimsical land.
Float along this starry spree,
Where humor's the key to set it free.

Enigmas of the Expanse

Mysteries lurk among bright tides,
With goofy moons on their wild rides.
Aliens giggle, green eyes aglow,
As they ponder what we don't know.

Nebulas swirl in colors bold,
Creating tales that never get old.
Fuzzy logic in a distant sphere,
Brings laughter closer, far yet near.

Black holes joke about their fate,
Swallowing stars, they cannot wait.
Comets giggle as they zoom by,
A cosmic vaudeville, oh my sky!

Between the galaxies, and the stars,
Laughter echoes from afar.
Join the fun, it's all a game,
In the vast unknown, we're all the same.

The Poetic Pulse

In rings of gas, we spin and twirl,
Like dancing fools, we give a whirl.
With moonbeams bouncing, a cosmic show,
Our laughter echoes, as we all glow.

Jupiter's big, but we steal the scene,
With funky vibes and a color scheme.
We'll juggle comets, and laugh out loud,
As we become the craziest crowd.

Stardust laughter, a silly spree,
If space were a circus, we'd hang from a tree.
Float through the cosmos, joyfully mad,
We're the coolest and silliest brigade.

In cosmic cafes, we swirl our cups,
With milky whirlpools, and intergalactic pups.
So grab a partner, let's laugh till we drop,
In this whirling universe, we just can't stop!

Vortex of Verses

Check out my moves, I'm lightyears ahead,
 Spinning like planets, let joy spread.
 In this word vortex, we twirl and sway,
  A cosmic ballet that's here to stay.

My rhymes are rings that glitter and gleam,
 Like chocolate sundaes in a wild dream.
  Shooting stars spin too fast to see,
   They dance on a whim, just like me!

If gravity's heavy, then we'll float light,
 Bubblegum dreams in the shimmering night.
  Choreographed chaos, smiles all around,
 In this cosmic whirl, we're bound to astound!

So twinkle your fingers, make wishes so sweet,
 In this galaxy funk, there's no defeat.
With verse in our pockets, let's play and cheer,
 For each cosmic note brings us all near!

Echoes of the Ecliptic

Echoes bounce 'round in cosmic space,
A chorus of chuckles in stellar embrace.
We're giggling comets on a wild skate,
Flipping through orbits, it's never too late.

With every pun, we discover and play,
Like crumbling asteroids in a wacky ballet.
We'll blow up the myths, tickle the fears,
With laughter resounding across the years.

In the shadow of giants, we hop like mad,
Galaxy travelers, each one a tad.
A carnival ride on a thunderous star,
Our echoes ring out, no matter how far.

Spin the globe, give it a slap,
In this comet band, we're taking a lap.
So join in the fun, let your spirits fly,
With each echoing laugh, we'll touch the sky!

Twilight Transmissions

In twilight's glow, we send our cheer,
Cosmic messages, celestial and clear.
Whimsical whispers on the evening breeze,
Riding the starlight, with effortless ease.

Barrels of laughter, we roll through the night,
Our rhymes spin magic, so dazzlingly bright.
With cosmic puns that could make you swoon,
Dance to the rhythm of the giggling moon.

Through asteroid fields, we'll skip and bound,
In this galactic playground, joy's all around.
So grab your glow sticks, let's rave with flair,
In this twilight party, we'll dazzle the air.

Each burst of laughter is a star on the rise,
Tickling stardust in the vast, open skies.
With echoes of joy, we beam from afar,
In these twilight transmissions, we're the shining stars!

Dark Matter Melodies

In the void where voices play,
Invisible tunes drift and sway.
Black holes chuckle, swirling round,
Lost in laughter, not a sound.

Galaxies dance, a cosmic spree,
Wobbling stars—what could they be?
Gravity jokes pulled tight and snug,
Pull my leg, then give a shrug.

Planets spin like tops at play,
Orbiting humor every day.
With dark matter, we all conspire,
Fueling laughter, a cosmic fire.

In this realm, we all have fun,
Chasing shadows, avoiding the sun.
Jokes in orbit, with no regret,
In this dark, we're not done yet!

Rhythms of the Roaming Realm

In the realm where comets race,
Their tails swirl like they own the place.
Meteor showers, a confetti blast,
Laughter echoes, the die is cast.

Asteroids bump in a wobbly waltz,
Dancing to rhythms that never halt.
They crash with glee, a playful spree,
Making friends with space debris.

Planets tease in their looping loops,
Joking about their distant troops.
A Saturn ring toss in the night,
Grand prizes—just not in sight!

Across this sphere, the laughter swells,
Witty jests? They outshine spells.
In the roaming realm, joy's the theme,
Together spinning, we all beam!

Celestial Chorus

Stars in clusters sing a song,
Melodies echo, joyfully strong.
Shooting stars weave tales of mirth,
Bringing giggles to the earth.

Luna winks from her silver throne,
Guiding wishes with a playful tone.
Voices rise in a cosmic hymn,
As comets dance and planets grin.

In the skies, there's no need to fret,
With a chorus we won't forget.
Galaxies join in, harmonize,
Creating laughter that never dies.

In this celestial show of glee,
Every note sets our spirits free.
Join the chorus, let's take flight,
Singing joy into the night!

Starlit Sequences

Count the stars, what a sight,
Each one laughs, glowing bright.
Patterns emerge in playful ways,
Sketching smiles through endless days.

Twinkling sprinkles of cosmic cheer,
Sending giggles from far and near.
A sequence of jokes, so divine,
Wrapped in starlight, how they shine!

Orbits twist, and jests unfold,
Stories of laughter, witty, bold.
In each shimmer, a tale to tell,
Starlit secrets, we know them well.

So gaze up at the night so grand,
With every twinkle, lend a hand.
In the starlit sequences we find,
Laughter ties us, heart and mind!

Tides of Time and Space

In cosmic dance, the planets spin,
Time ticks away, where to begin?
A comet sneezed, and off it went,
Caught in a loop, a cosmic event.

The stars they laugh, a twinkling crew,
Forgetting earthlings, who've lost their shoe.
Galaxies gossip, they nod and swirl,
While we take selfies and give it a whirl.

Black holes yawn, their appetites grand,
Swallowing light, isn't that just bland?
Yet still we send probes to the void,
Hoping for signals, perhaps just a ploy.

Space is a joke, we play the fool,
We thought we were wise, just look at the rule!
Planets are partying, spinning with glee,
What a messy, funny cosmic jubilee!

Resonance of the Rings

Oh those rings, they shimmer and shine,
Made of dust, oh isn't that fine?
Planets with bling, a celestial show,
Who needs style? Just watch them glow!

They jiggle and bounce, a wobbly dance,
Caught in the cosmos, it's pure happenstance.
Meteorites throw confetti with flair,
As comets crash through, without a care!

We humans debate, what do they mean?
A fashion statement or just for the scene?
The rings only laugh, a cosmic delight,
"Wear what you want, it's all outta sight!"

They're poets in orbit, a swirling ballet,
With verses of stardust, they drift and sway.
In laughter they bask, amidst the space woes,
A cosmic comedy, the universe knows!

The Poetic Infinity

In the vastness, an echo of glee,
Time stretches out, as wide as can be.
Aliens giggle, with tentacled glee,
What's a rhyme? Let's just shake the tree!

Verses unwritten, in cosmic graffiti,
Words lost in black holes, oh what a pity!
"Yo! Send a postcard from the great beyond,
We'll be here spinning, of life we're so fond!"

Infinity laughs in a humor so sly,
Like a clown in a nebula, oh my oh my!
Infinity's a joke, where nothing makes sense,
Planets in jest, no need for pretense.

We scribble our thoughts on stardust pages,
While comets roll by, like funny stage sages.
In this poetic void, we toss rhymes around,
In the realm of the cosmos, laughter is found!

Whispers of the Wandering Planets

Wandering planets, oh what a sight,
They drift and they laugh, in the soft moonlight.
A jovial Jupiter, king of the show,
Sings silly tunes, as he goes with the flow.

Mars tells a joke, "I'm red because,"
"Earth's just green with envy, when we land on her buzz"

Venus rolls eyes, feeling so hot,
"Stop making me blush, it's all I've got!"

Neptune waves gaily, a blue ocean bore,
"Your jokes are too dry, come dance on my floor!"
Pluto just pouts, "Am I a planet still?"
But laughter erupts, he's got charm and will!

In the vastness, the whispers unfold,
With giggles and quirks, in stories untold.
Wandering planets, they are quite the crew,
In this cosmic comedy, we're laughing with you!

The Language of Light

Bright beams are chatting, oh so sly,
Photons dancing, they zoom and fly.
Wavelengths whisper secrets so sweet,
In a cosmic café, they laugh and greet.

Shining jokes in every hue,
Light's got puns, it's true, it's true.
Twinkling stars in a playful jest,
Making dark matter chuckle, no less!

In this spectrum of giggles we roam,
Radiant rascals, they're far from home.
Laughter echoes through the vast expanse,
Every sparkle a wink, a silly glance.

The universe beams in vibrant tones,
Crafting humor with cosmic drones.
So let's toast with rays of delight,
In this party of photons, everything's bright!

Verses of the Void

In the deep where silence reigns,
The void holds echoes of silly refrains.
Galactic jokes and comets with flair,
Spinning tales in the cold, dark air.

Black holes giggle, pulling us near,
With a gravitational tug and a cheer.
Lost in a chuckle, where time drips slow,
Like a milkshake in space, all crazy flow.

Asteroids stumble, tripping through night,
Laughing at planets, oh what a sight!
Craters are punchlines, no sharp edges there,
Just humorous happenings floating with flare.

Oh, the void is a canvas for laughter to bloom,
In the absence of light, there's still room!
So here's to the silence, let's revel in glee,
For funny is found where the wonders must be!

Interstellar Improv

On a stage made of stardust, bright and bold,
Actors in orbits, their antics unfold.
Space-time jokes, with a twist and a turn,
Galactic giggles for all who yearn.

Comets improvise lines with a swoosh,
Playing tag with the planets in a cosmic push.
Neptune's bluing grins, Saturn's rings jive,
Laughter fuels rockets, keeping dreams alive.

Each star a performer, each quasar a muse,
In the theater of cosmos, there's no chance to snooze!
Curtains of nebulae drape soft in the glow,
As laughter erupts in an interstellar flow.

So bring on the laughter, let creativity reign,
In a universe bursting with humor and gain.
The cosmos applauds with a dazzling light,
As we improvise laughter in the dark of the night!

The Untamed Universe

In the wilds of space, anything goes,
A supernova giggles as it blows.
Planets take flights on jokes made of gas,
Laughing at comets as they zip past.

Galaxies whirl in a chaotic dance,
Shaking their arms to an astral romance.
Stardust confetti rains down from the sky,
While quasars beam bright with a wink and a sigh.

With meteors racing like bumblebees,
And time having fun, bending like trees.
Eclipses are spectacles, nature's own gags,
As the universe plays with its playful rags.

So let's celebrate with a cosmic cheer,
In this untamed playground, there's nothing to fear.
For laughter's the gravity, our hearts entwine,
In the amazing vastness, we all shine divine!

Celestial Cadence

In the cosmic dance, I trip and fall,
Got my space boots on, cruising through it all,
Bumped into Mars, gave him a wink,
He shrugged and said, 'Hey, it's not what you think.'

Galaxies swirl, and I'm sipping my drink,
Asteroids tumbling, I'm starting to sink,
"Watch out!" I shout, as I dodge a moon,
The universe laughs, its wild, crazy tune.

Planets align with a playful little grin,
It's just stardust, let the fun begin!
Lost in the orbits, where laughter's the way,
Dancing on rings, oh what a display!

So gather your friends, let the orbits spin,
In this cosmic party, we're all in to win,
From black holes to novas, we'll make the scene,
In the vastness of space, we're the sparkling beam.

Rings of Rhetoric

Riding the rings, I'm feeling the beat,
Words like comets, they glide on my feet,
"Did you hear Jupiter's got a new coat?"
I chuckle aloud, while the stardust floats.

Conversations swirl, in the middle of space,
My witty retorts are winning the race,
Venus just winked, the sun's feeling bright,
And I'm crafting my lines under soft moonlight.

Dropping some rhymes like meteors crash,
They land with a punch, but fade in a flash,
Eclipsing the haters with a stellar surprise,
My verses are diamonds that light up the skies.

So let's toast to the cosmos, a gathering place,
Turn up the volume, let's rock the vast space,
In a whirl of laughter, we'll rise and we'll cheer,
With rings of good vibes that we'll all hold dear.

Cosmic Verses Untangled

Floating through galaxies, my thoughts all jumbled,
Each verse wraps around like I've really fumbled,
"Hey, Uranus, got a joke for the day?"
He chuckles back, "Only if I can stay!"

From quarks to quasars, I flip and I spin,
Spitting out bars with a sly little grin,
Pluto's just hanging, still in the mix,
Shaking his head, saying, "I'm not in the fix."

Stellar puns collide, exploding in space,
Galactic giggles put a smile on my face,
With asteroids laughing as they zoom by,
I cradle the cosmos and let out a sigh.

So let's weave the stardust and laughter tonight,
In whispers of nebulae, we'll take flight,
Through waves of humor in this boundless domain,
Cosmic verses untangled, let's dance in the rain.

Echoes from the Gas Giant

Echoes are bouncing in a loud, fun spree,
Gassy with laughter, just come join me,
Floating on breezes that tickle and tease,
Comedic explosions, I'm down on my knees!

Bounding on clouds, like a balloon gone wild,
"Did you hear the one about that starry-eyed child?"
Sipping on starlight, I take a deep breath,
Words flowing freely, no fear of regret.

In this jovial chaos, we twist and we swirl,
Every quip an adventure, every joke a whirl,
From the rings of delight to the jokes in the mist,
I'm juggling my laughs – can't let any go missed!

So gather your giggles, and let's not be shy,
In this gas giant kingdom, we'll reach for the sky,
With echoes of joy that will never depart,
Launching our humor, straight into the heart.

Whispers of the Orbital Storm

In the dance of cosmic quirks,
Rings like hula hoops, they jerk.
Planets spin, they trip and glide,
Swirling chaos, in joy we ride.

Asteroids wearing funky hats,
Dodging moons like playful cats.
Galaxies with winks and pouts,
Eclipses chuckle, no doubts.

Uranus slips on a silly shoe,
Jupiter's laugh echoes, it's true!
Comets swoosh with glitter trails,
In this storm, we all are pals.

So let us swirl in cosmic cheer,
With laughter that we hold so dear.
In the storm of laughs we thrive,
Dancing 'round, oh how we jive!

The Rhythm of the Ringed World

Bouncing notes in a spacey jam,
Rings like tambourines, oh man!
Jupiter beats with thunderous drum,
While Mars performs a dance of fun.

Neptune winks in electric blue,
Dancing stars in a swirling hue.
Satellites giggle, orbiting fast,
In this cosmic bash, we all are cast.

Melodies of planets in sync,
With cosmic riffs that make you think.
Stardust showers, twinkling smack,
Hit that beat, there's no lack!

Gravity holds us while we sway,
Moving to the fresh Milky Way.
In this ringed world, we take our stand,
With laughter from every corner of the land.

Interstellar Expressions

In the vastness, expressions fly,
Planets blush as comets cry.
Stars wink like they've got a joke,
In the void, a laughter cloak.

Aliens giggle at our Earth ways,
Doing the worm in a cosmic haze.
Voyager whispers sweet nothings low,
To galaxies that put on a show.

Supernovas pop like confetti spark,
While black holes pull us into the dark.
But we resist their serious plight,
With smiles that shine, oh so bright!

Interstellar wit weaves through space,
Chasing laughter at a rapid pace.
In this boundless cosmic field,
Silly secrets are revealed!

Gravity's Gravitational Grief

Gravity pulls, oh what a tease,
Holding us down like a cosmic sneeze.
Planets grumble, but can't escape,
In this tug of war, they shape.

Space-time jests like a funny old clown,
With jokes that whirl us round and round.
Stars hit the floor with a playful bounce,
In this universe, we all can pounce.

Floating dreams in zero G,
We're weightless, oh can't you see?
Laugh away the cosmic strife,
In gravity's arms, we find our life.

So hold on tight to that giggle fit,
Even when the pull won't quit.
In the dance of forces, strong and bright,
We laugh it off, take flight, take flight!

Celestial Musings

In orbit, I twirl, feeling quite spry,
With rings made of ice, oh my, oh my!
Asteroids laugh, they dance in a spin,
While planets whisper, 'Can we join in?'

Jupiter's storms throw quite the bash,
While Neptune's blues give a splashy splash.
I juggle comets, with style and flair,
An interstellar act, beyond compare!

Galaxies giggle, they twinkle with glee,
Shooting stars ask, "What's next for me?"
With a wink and a nudge, they tease the night,
As I sip stardust, feeling just right!

Space is a stage, we're all in the scene,
With meteors crashing, like none have seen.
So let's raise a toast to the cosmic show,
Where laughter erupts, and good vibes flow!

Cadence of the Cosmos

In the rhythm of space, I dance all around,
With pulsars pulsing a beat so profound.
Planets bounce like they're on a trampoline,
While black holes giggle: 'We're the unseen!'

Supernovae burst like a pop star's song,
Each twinkle a note, where we all belong.
I tap my feet on the Milky Way's rim,
And laugh with the moons, our lights never dim.

Venus struts in a dazzling glow,
While Mercury zips like a comet in tow.
I'm spinning with joy, my heart takes flight,
In the dance of the cosmos, everything's right!

With asteroid friends, we twirl side to side,
Creating a melody, as we glide.
So join in the fun, let's make a parade,
In this cosmic concert, we all serenade!

Rhythmic Revolutions

Swirling and twirling, a cosmic ballet,
With meteoric mischief on display.
I flip like a fish in a space ocean wide,
While Saturn chuckles: 'I'm ready to ride!'

Neptune's blue waves, they're rolling with glee,
As I bounce to the beat, just feeling so free.
Asteroids chant, 'We're here for the fun!'
While comets zoom by, they're never outdone!

Galactic giggles echo through night,
As meteor showers create such delight.
With starlight confetti, we party for days,
In the rhythm of space, a wild, joyful craze!

Join me in laughter, as we orbit and spin,
In the dance of the heavens, let the fun begin!
With the universe laughing, it's truly a win,
Caught up in the magic, and wearing a grin!

The Language of Light Years

In light years we chat, with giggles and glee,
We wink at the sun, like we're all family.
I tell the stars jokes, they sparkle with joy,
Planetary punchlines that none can destroy!

With quasars shining bright, they join in my rhyme,
Creating a laughter that stretches through time.
Each photon a word, each light beam a cheer,
As we spin through this cosmos, designed without fear!

Galaxies sharing the funniest tales,
While gravity's pull often unveils,
A universe filled with wonders so grand,
In this cosmic comedy, hand in hand!

So let's play with stardust, let's laugh with the night,
In the language of cosmos, everything's bright.
Embrace the absurd, let's all take a bow,
For humor in space, it's happening now!

Nebula Nights

In the cosmic glow, we sip our tea,
Stars twinkling like disco, come dance with me.
Galaxies giggle, the comets pursue,
Under the blanket of shimmering blue.

Wormholes wave, they ask me to twirl,
Astrophysicists' heads start to swirl.
With cosmic confetti that comes from afar,
We'll spin in the shadows of a giant star.

Planets parade in this space-age spree,
Jupiter jumps, and Mercury's free.
In the laughter of the void, we lose all care,
Moonbeams mix drinks; it's a party up there!

Quasars quip in a stellar play,
While supernovae burst, taking boredom away.
With every burst, a new joke will rise,
In this universe where humor defies.

Pulses of the Planet

Hey there, Earth, you're looking quite round,
Spinning and laughing, a joyful sound.
Your crusty old surface, so full of cheer,
Turns up the volume, let all planets hear!

The Moon's cracking jokes, it's quite the delight,
With a humor so lunar, it'll keep you up night.
Pluto chimes in, though he's now a dwarf,
Says, "But I'm the funniest, so what's your worth?"

Venus fumes, hot like a flaming red hat,
Mumbling to Mars, "What's up with that?"
While Saturn just laughs, rings clinking like bells,
In this cosmic comedy where all humor dwells.

Uranus rolls in with a cheeky little grin,
Saying "Let's get wacky, let the fun begin!"
Bodies that bounce, in a space hop parade,
Join the laughter and let the gloom fade.

Asteroid Anthems

Bouncing off rocks in an asteroid field,
Singing sweet tunes, our hearts are revealed.
Chunky old boulders grooving with flair,
Every collision's a dance, we don't really care!

With each little impact, a rhythm appears,
In the silence of space, we drown out our fears.
A melody echoes, no stars up ahead,
In the playful pull of a celestial thread.

Rolling through orbits, dodging and spinning,
With laughter as fuel, this jam will be winning.
They call us space rocks, but we're dancers at heart,
In the cosmic cabaret, we all play a part.

So gather your friends from a belt far away,
Join the asteroid chorus; let's laugh and sway.
In a universe filled with splinters and laughs,
Our catchy little tunes bring cosmic sweet gaffs.

Gravity's Groove

In the sweet tug of gravity, we sway and spin,
Floating like feathers, we dance with a grin.
You drop your keys—oh dear, what a plight,
But pick them up dancing, it feels so right!

The pull of the planet, it's hard to resist,
But swirling with laughter, you won't want to miss.
In this funky ballet, we leap and we dive,
With giggles galore, oh, we're truly alive!

With moons that boogie and suns that sway,
The cosmos is groovy; come join us, okay?
Let's float through the cosmos with joyous delight,
Chasing the stars till we've danced out of sight.

So lift your spirits, just sway with the flow,
Let the beats of the cosmos put on a show.
In this hilarious dance, we're all in the zone,
With gravity's grip, we'll never be alone!

Rhythmic Stardust

In the sky with a twinkle, it's a dance of glee,
Planets groove, oh what a sight to see!
Jupiter jumps with a laugh so bright,
While Mercury zips, always ready to fight.

Neptune whispers, 'Just chill, my friend,'
While Venus struts like it's a fashion trend.
Mars throws a party, it's out of sight,
With asteroids rockin' all through the night.

Echoes from Beyond

Echoes ricochet in the cosmic air,
A cosmic joke is floating everywhere.
Black holes giggle with a troll-like stealth,
Swallowing stars and munching on wealth.

Twinkling lights send an interstellar text,
'Hey, Earthlings, hear this, we're not perplexed!'
Comets come by on their wild chase,
As humor swirls in this vast, vast space.

The Dance of the Cosmos

Planets waltz through the Milky Way,
Galloping comets join in the play.
With cosmic rhythms, they twirl and spin,
Chasing gravity—they all want to win!

Moonbeams chuckle as they pass so near,
Shooting stars throw wishes, hey, let's cheer!
In this galactic jive, there's never a lull,
They're spinning and laughing—oh, isn't it cool?

Celestial Circles

Galaxies swirl in a dizzy embrace,
Light-years apart, yet face to face.
Comedy cosmic, with each quirky star,
Lighting up laughter, no matter how far.

Planets play tag on an orbital spree,
While aliens chuckle, 'Look, that's just me!'
In circles we laugh, harmonious and bright,
In this funny universe, all is just right.

Starlight Stanzas

In the sky where the planets dance,
A ringed giant winks at a chance.
His moons giggle as they twirl around,
Making merry in the vastness found.

Last night a comet tripped on grace,
And all the stars burst into space.
They laughed and sparkled, a galactic jest,
While the cosmic dust debated who's best.

Each nebula whispers a silly caught tale,
Of black holes that gulp and comets that sail.
In this universe, humor's the key,
Where gravity's pull is a giggle, you see!

So join the fun with a jovial cheer,
As the astral beings raise a toast here.
For every twinkle and wink from above,
Is a cosmic reminder, we're all made of love.

Astral Adventures

Through stardust trails and laughter sprawl,
Jupiter's storms are the best type of brawl.
His Great Red Spot spins a yarn so divine,
While his moons share jokes over celestial wine.

Mars threw a party, but the rovers just stood,
'Is it fun? Will I fall? Is it all good?'
Venus popped in with a hot, sultry glow,
'Let's spice it up, come on, let's go!'

Neptune's laugh echoed far and wide,
As he rapped in the rings, a galactic guide.
With lyrics and rhythms so cool and so bright,
Even the asteroids danced through the night.

So strap in tight for this stellar ride,
Where laughter's the fuel in the cosmic tide.
Adventure awaits in the skies so grand,
With playful spirits that always expand.

Cosmic Conversations

In the vacuum, two asteroids met,
'What's the gossip?' one asked, with no regret.
The other replied with a chuckle so bold,
'The rings of a giant have stories untold!'

Stars gossip over cosmic tea,
'Have you heard what the black hole said to me?'
'I'll swallow your secrets, just watch me appear,
And I'll leave you in darkness, my dear!'

A supernova joined in with a grin,
'Why don't we all let the fun begin?
We'll burst into laughter across the void,
And paint this bleak universe, newly enjoyed!'

So here we float in the endless abyss,
With light-hearted banter and comets amiss.
In this cosmic café, let's sip and delight,
Sharing dreams that dance in the endless night.

Infinity's Ink

On a parchment of stars, I scribble some fate,
With ink made of stardust and laughter innate.
A tale of a planet who tripped on a rock,
And got tangled in rings like some cosmic clock.

Or how a lost comet took a detour for fun,
Only to find that he's not the only one.
He met a space whale with a penchant for jokes,
And together they laughed, two quirky folks.

In this ink of infinity, tales twist and play,
The universe chuckles in a spectacular way.
For every quasar that blinks with delight,
Is a reminder that humor ignites the night.

So pen those stories that sparkle and gleam,
Fill the cosmos with laughter, each whimsical dream.
In this vast expanse, let your spirit unwind,
As you dance with the stars – leave your woes behind.

Gravity's Grasp

In the cosmos, I sway and dance,
Floating freely, no need for pants.
With each step, I laugh and twirl,
Who knew space could be such a whirl?

Invisible strings pull me here and there,
Trying to catch me? Just don't dare!
I swing through the stars like a kid on a slide,
Gravity's grasp is a wild ride!

Planets are spinning, it's hard to keep track,
I've lost my lunch; it's floating back!
With laughter echoing across the night,
Cosmic clowns bring new delight!

So here's a toast to the celestial show,
Adrift in the universe, go with the flow.
With a wink to the whirls we all partake,
Let's spin through the cosmos, for laughter's sake!

The Dancer of Distant Orbits

A dancer spins on rings of ice,
Twisting through space, oh so nice.
With sparkles in her hair, she sways,
Inventing new moves in a cosmic haze.

She winks at Jupiter, shimmies the sun,
Galactic dance-offs are just so much fun!
With planets clapping and comets that cheer,
Every far-off world can't help but appear!

Her twirls create whirlpools of joy and glee,
Each movement vibrant, wild, and free.
She laughs as she steps on a meteor's tail,
Leaving behind a glittering trail.

So watch her as she plays with the night,
A cosmic ballet, a marvelous sight.
In the realm where stars and planets align,
The dancer of orbits is simply divine!

Whispering Moons

Oh, the moons gather round in a silvery chat,
Sharing their secrets, imagine that!
"Did you see that comet?" one moon chimed in,
"It flashed by so fast, looked like a win!"

They giggle and gossip in a hushed tone,
As meteor showers are brightly shown.
"Mars still thinks he's the hottest of all,
But have you seen Venus? She's got the ball!"

The whispers float light in the cosmic air,
Twinkling thoughts in a starlit affair.
"Let's prank the asteroids, make them spin,
We'll light up the night and dance, join in!"

So the moons keep their laughter, a cosmic delight,
Their giggles echo through the endless night.
With tales of the skies, in joy they croon,
Forever united, the whispering moons!

Titan's Tantalizing Tale

On Titan's shores, the waves do crash,
A spectacle rich, a vibrant splash!
Creatures emerge with a grin so wide,
"Join us for fun, let's take a ride!"

With bubbles of methane in colors so bright,
Swimmers leap in, a hilarious sight.
"Watch out!" one yells as he trips on the sand,
"I'm the best diver in this alien land!"

The atmosphere thick, but spirits are high,
Dancers do flips beneath the purple sky.
"It's colder than Earth, but who needs a breeze?
With laughter and joy, we make our own Leez!"

So join in the merriment, sail through the haze,
Titan's tale tickles in zany displays.
With each liquid ripple, the fun never fails,
Come hear the laughter in Titan's bright trails!

www.ingramcontent.com/pod-product-compliance
Lightning Source LLC
Chambersburg PA
CBHW072145200426
43209CB00051B/717